IDEAS AND INVENTIONS

GENERATING POWER

Turning Science into Energy

Philip Wilkinson

Illustrated by Robert Ingpen

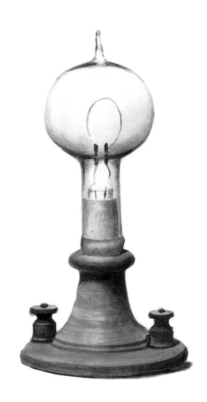

Chrysalis Children's Books

First published in the UK in 2005 by
Chrysalis Children's Books
An imprint of Chrysalis Books Group Plc,
The Chrysalis Building, Bramley Road, London W10 6SP

Text copyright © Philip Wilkinson 2005
Illustrations copyright © Robert Ingpen 1997, 2005

ISBN   1 84458 212 4

British Library Cataloguing in Publication Data
for this book is available from the British Library.

Editorial Manager: Joyce Bentley
Senior Editor: Rasha Elsaeed
Series Editor: Jon Richards
Editorial Assistant: Camilla Lloyd
Designed by: Tall Tree Ltd
Cover Make-up: Wladek Szechter

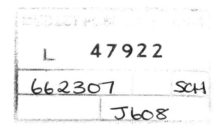

Previously published in four volumes for Dragon's World *Caves to Cathedrals, Science & Power, Scrolls to Computers* and *Wheels to Rockets*.

Printed in China

10 9 8 7 6 5 4 3 2 1

CONTENTS

Introduction

Today we are surrounded by machines. We travel in cars and on trains, we have devices like cranes to lift heavy weights, our factories are full of machines that help us to make things. However, a few thousand years ago life was very different. People walked everywhere or rode animals, heavy items had to be lifted by hand and everything had to be made using the simplest of tools. Most jobs took much longer to complete, and involved a lot of sheer hard work. A big project like putting up a building needed a small army of labourers to carry stone, lift wooden beams and fix everything in place.

These ancient builders were using the most basic form of power – the power of their own muscles. They only had very simple machines, such as ramps or pulleys, to help them. Eventually, however, people began to discover other sources of power. Looking at a fast-flowing stream, they realised that they could use the power of the water to turn a wheel and drive machinery – they had come up with the idea of the water mill. By building windmills they could use the

power of the wind in a similar way. So for hundreds of years, water mills and windmills were used to power machinery for all sorts of jobs – from grinding corn to make flour to sawing wood.

Wind and water were incredibly useful, but in the nineteenth century, engineers discovered an even more reliable source of power – electricity – which could be used in everything from factory machinery to lights in the home. It caught on slowly to begin with, because it took years to lay the cables to connect houses and factories up with the power stations

where electricity was generated. But by the middle of the twentieth century, vast areas of the world were connected and people could get access to power, just as we do today, by simply flicking a switch.

When scientists discovered how to produce electricity by nuclear reactions, it seemed as if the world at last had a cheap and endless supply of energy. However, nuclear power carries enormous risks. So today's scientists are developing new ways of generating energy from natural sources of power – for example, from the Sun and the waves. The story of generating power has a fascinating future ahead.

PHILIP WILKINSON

What is Power?

n this book, the word 'power' is used to describe the way in which a basic source of energy is exploited to help us do things. There are several different kinds of power. When you lift a book off a shelf or open a door you are using the power of your own muscles. When you ride a horse, you are travelling by animal muscle power and the machinery in a water mill or windmill is moved by natural power. Most of the gadgets in your home are probably driven by electricity, but this electricity can be generated in all sorts of ways, from the movement of water, for example, or through the process of a nuclear reaction.

When you go riding, you have to harness your horse, so that you can control the animal as it moves. The harness helps you tell the horse when to stop and start, when to speed up or slow down, when to turn and when to carry on in a straight line. Every source of power has to be tapped and controlled in this way in order to make it usable by people, and scientists talk about 'harnessing' a source of power.

To harness wind power you need a windmill, while to harness the power of petrol you need a car with an internal combustion engine.

The whole story of technology is about inventors working out how to harness different kinds of power. The first true factories were only possible because engineers invented ways of harnessing steam power by building steam engines in the nineteenth century. Cars were made possible because of the development of gas and petrol engines more than one hundred years ago. And devices like the latest computers and games machines can only work because scientists in the past worked out how to harness electricity.

Everything in your house took power to produce. The furniture may have been made using electrically powered machine tools, a picture on the wall may have been painted using muscle power – but the canvas was probably woven on an electric loom. So power is everywhere, in everything we do and everything we own. It is one of the most important forces, both in history and in our everyday lives.

MACHINE POWER

The story of machines began thousands of years ago when ancient people devised easier ways to lift heavy weights, split building stone and move objects from one place to another.

From the simplest man-powered machines, such as the wheelbarrow or the pulley, to complex powered machines, such as the car, all machines are tools that make work easier.

We know from prehistoric sites such as Stonehenge in England, built around

△ Wooden levers can be used to help raise a heavy weight.

◁ The simplest machines, such as wedges for splitting rocks, mean that strenuous tasks can be performed with less effort.

about 3000 BC, that amazing feats of moving and lifting were carried out using only human and perhaps animal power. No one is sure exactly what methods were used to carry the huge blocks of stone necessary, but rollers, levers and wedges must have played a part. Even with the help of these devices, building projects such as the great cities of ancient Persia and Egypt took thousands of people many years to build.

WEDGES FOR BUILDING
The ancient Egyptians used wedges in a wide variety of ways. In building, they

MACHINE POWER

▷*Machines did not only help in manufacturing and building work. This catapult is a type of lever. It was used to throw heavy or burning objects over a wall during a siege.*

often trimmed a piece of stone to a wedge shape and then drove it between other stones to make a tight fit. They used sloping wedges as ramps for pushing stone into place. In raising stone columns, or 'obelisks', they lowered the base into position down a slope, and then used ropes tied around the top to haul the obelisk upright.

The Egyptians also used wedges to split stone. They drilled holes in blocks of stone and then hammered in wooden wedges. Water was poured on to the wood, which made it expand, splitting the stone.

THE POWER OF THE LEVER

The lever was another of the simple machines available to ancient people. We use levers many times every day without realizing it. Every time we open a door, cut with scissors or play on a see-saw, we are making use of levers. Although ancient peoples did not understand the

principle of how levers work, they used them for many tasks. The oar is a kind of lever, as is the wheelbarrow.

In the third century BC, the Greek scientist Archimedes (287–212 BC) began to experiment with levers and figured out how to make them do the most work for the least effort. Archimedes wrote that if he were given a lever long enough and a place to stand, he could move the whole Earth. This was just a fantasy, of course, but it suggested the lever's power.

It was soon discovered that the feet could operate levers in the form of treadles, leaving the hands free for other tasks. Treadles were used to operate hammers for pounding rice into flour, and in weaving machines. Most of the devices we use in the modern world, from cars to electric light switches, contain levers. The clutch, brake and accelerator pedals of a car are all treadle-type levers.

ROUND AND ROUND, UP AND DOWN

Changing a rotary, or round-and-round, effort into a lifting or pulling effort was a challenge that the machine-makers of the ancient world faced, and beat.

Although we know the device described by Archimedes for raising water as the 'Archimedes screw', he was writing about a machine that he had seen rather than one he had invented. The screw can be thought of as a slope arranged in a spiral. When the handle of the Archimedes screw was turned by human or animal power, the thread of the screw carried water up the shaft.

In a similar way, turning a screw to fasten two pieces of wood converts the rotary motion of the screwdriver into a linear motion which pulls the two pieces of wood together. When gear wheels are cut so that they mesh together, they can have the same effect of changing the direction of effort.

SCREWING IT UP

The screw is another ancient device. We think of it today mainly as a way of fastening wood or metal, but the screw as a fastener did not become widespread until the eighteenth century. Until then, it was not possible to make screw threads accurately enough.

The ancient world used the screw in quite different ways. A screw is, in fact, a slope or inclined plane which winds around in a spiral. Archimedes described such a screw device for raising water to irrigate fields, but this had been in use long before his time. The Greeks and Romans used screws in presses to extract juice and oil from grapes and olives.

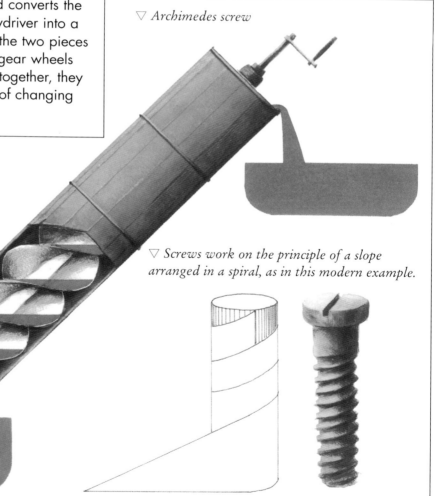

▽ *Archimedes screw*

▽ *Screws work on the principle of a slope arranged in a spiral, as in this modern example.*

THE PULLEY

In a pulley, a rope lifting a load is passed between two or more grooved wheels. Passing the rope over one pulley makes the task of lifting easier, but using two or more is even more effective. The ancient Greeks are known to have used a system of pulleys to haul rock from a silver mine.

The crane was a development of the pulley. It had a long arm called a 'jib' which carried the pulleys. The jib was mounted on a platform which could be revolved, and worked by a treadmill operated by human power. The crane was possibly first developed by the Romans as a machine for loading and unloading cargoes from ships.

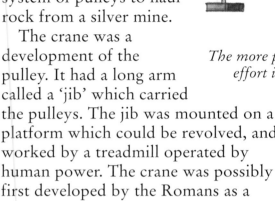

The more pulleys there are, the less effort it takes to lift a load.

THE WINCH

Another hauling and lifting machine invented in early times was the winch. A rope tied to a load passed over a horizontal wooden roller which was operated by a handle. As the handle turned, the rope wound around it, dragging the load nearer. A winch was used in a copper mine in Austria around 600 BC. A similar device with a vertical roller is called a windlass. The ancient Egyptians used a windlass operated by ox power to lift water from rivers in jars and transfer it to irrigation channels.

After the collapse of the Roman Empire, there was no large-scale building in Europe for about 500 years. There were no longer vast armies of slaves to do the lifting and pulling. However, in the late Middle Ages, the Christian church began to build new great cathedrals throughout western Europe. All the skills of engineers and builders were called upon, and the result was a revival of machines that were used in the past to handle the huge blocks of stone and heavy timbers that were needed.

SEA TRADING

When it was seen how effective these machines were, they found other uses, particularly at ports where the windlass became a valuable tool for pulling ships in close to the quays, and the crane for loading and unloading. At a time when trade by sea was increasing rapidly, machines that helped ship-owners to turn their ships around quickly were welcome. Ports with such equipment as cranes and winches attracted the trade, and their merchants grew prosperous alongside the ship-owners who used them.

THE FIRST MACHINE TOOLS

Meanwhile, simple machines had been developing in a completely different direction, in the making of machine tools. A machine tool is a device which helps to speed up repetitive but skilled tasks, such as cutting or shaping metal or wood.

The first machine tool was the potter's wheel. Before it was invented about 6,000 years ago, pots were made either by pressing clay over a rounded object or by building up a coil of clay and smoothing together the edges. The wheel, turned by a handle or a treadle, enabled pots to be 'thrown' by the fingers, building them up from a ball of clay as the wheel turned.

THE LATHE

One of the most basic machine tools, the lathe, works in much the same way, by working on an object as it turns. We do not know when the first lathes were used. A wooden bowl made using a lathe has been found dating from about 700 BC. Earlier Egyptian paintings show a kind of lathe being used. A cord wrapped round the object being turned is being pulled by one worker while the other uses a chisel to shape the work.

In the Middle Ages, pole lathes were often used. The cord was atttached to the top of a springy wooden pole and wound round the work to be turned. At the other end of the cord was a treadle. Foot pressure from the treadle and tension from the pole kept the work turning. The advantage of this design was that one person could operate it and do the shaping.

▽ *The winch combines the use of a roller with a lever to make lifting or pulling a heavy weight easier. Here a pair of Greeks are using a winch, coupled with a lever and a treadle (or foot lever) to dredge mud out of a harbour. It must have been very hard work!*

THE QUEST FOR PERPETUAL MOTION

By the late Middle Ages, the development of machine technology had gone about as far as it could go while the effort that went into operating machines had to come either from humans or from animals such as oxen or donkeys. Wind and water power could be harnessed for some purposes, such as grinding corn, but many operations had to be carried on continuously, whatever the weather or the flow of a river. There were now no huge armies of slaves to provide human power, as there had been in ancient Egypt or Rome, and even beasts of burden had to be fed and looked after.

This problem teased at the minds of inventors and scientists. Their understanding of the science of mechanics was not very clear. Many people tried to invent machines that, once started, would just keep going without any further energy being applied. These were called 'perpetual motion' machines. Such a device, they thought, could be used to operate levers, winches, pulleys and other simple machines for as long as it was needed.

They were wasting their time. Forces over which we have no control, such as friction and gravity, mean that any device with no external power source will eventually slow down and stop. Perpetual motion was not the answer to the problem of power, but it was not until the late eighteenth century, with the development of the steam engine, that a solution was found. Here are some of the proposed designs suggested in the impossible quest for a perpetual motion machine.

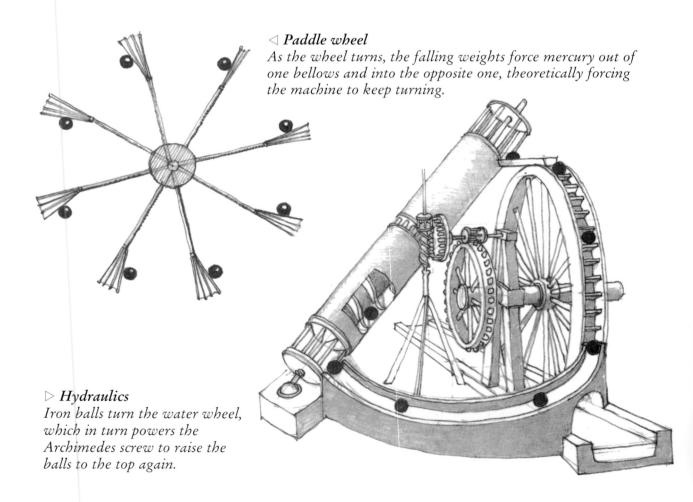

◁ *Paddle wheel*
As the wheel turns, the falling weights force mercury out of one bellows and into the opposite one, theoretically forcing the machine to keep turning.

▷ *Hydraulics*
Iron balls turn the water wheel, which in turn powers the Archimedes screw to raise the balls to the top again.

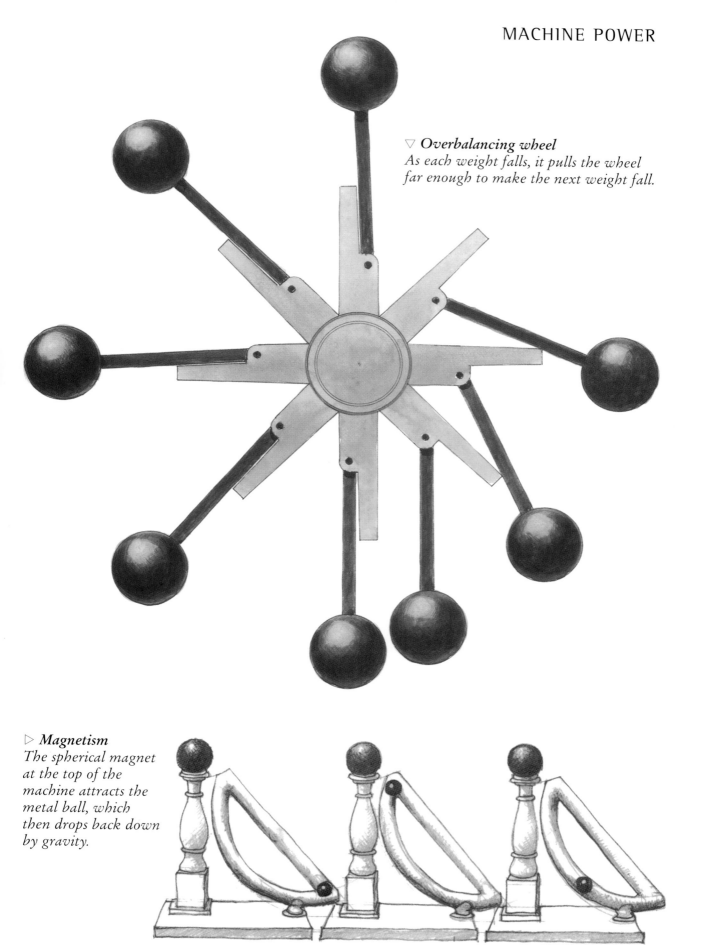

▽ **Overbalancing wheel**
As each weight falls, it pulls the wheel
far enough to make the next weight fall.

▷ **Magnetism**
The spherical magnet
at the top of the
machine attracts the
metal ball, which
then drops back down
by gravity.

MACHINE POWER

HE POWER HAMMER

The power hammer was a machine tool that reached Europe round about AD 1100, although it had been used in China at least 1,000 years before. It consisted of a heavy weight which was raised to a height above an anvil on which the object to be worked was placed. The weight was then released and allowed to drop by force of gravity.

The power hammer saved a great deal of effort when large numbers of similar items, such as sickle and knife blades, were needed. The first power hammers were driven by water-wheels.

DAWN OF A NEW AGE

At last, in the eighteenth century, engineers came up with something the world had been waiting for: a new way of powering machinery. The need for a breakthrough had become urgent, especially in Britain where there was a fuel crisis. Wood, either dried and burned or in the form of charcoal, had been Britain's main source of fuel, but the forests were being burned faster than they could be replanted.

As a result, people turned to coal, but this meant sinking pits deeper to levels where underground water flowed. The 'gin', a kind of windlass powered by horses, was used to drain the pits, but it did not work fast enough. Against this background, the steam engine was perfected by the Scottish engineer James Watt (1736–1819). Here was a source of power that could be used as a pumping engine, to help produce the fuel it

▷ *During the Middle Ages, machines began to make a difference to people's working lives. The machines used on this building site look basic to modern eyes, but they made building tasks possible which otherwise could only have been done with a huge army of workers.*

△ *Early steam engines were inefficient, but before long, steam revolutionized most industries.*

burned. Steam engines could also drive shafts that in turn could power all kinds of machine tools.

One of the problems with early steam engines was the fit between the piston and the cylinder in which it moved. If the piston was too loose, vital pressure was lost and the engine performed inefficiently. Attempts were made to seal the gap with rope or leather, but these seals quickly wore out.

CANNONS AND CYLINDERS

The solution to this problem was worked out by an English iron-founder, John Wilkinson (1728–1808). His main business was making armaments, including cannon barrels. Here too, there was a problem of fitting. Barrels too large for the cannon balls did not fire accurately. Barrels that were too small were likely to blow up when fired.

In 1774, Wilkinson invented a machine which gave his cannon barrels perfectly circular bores along all their length.

A hard cutting tool on the end of an iron bar was driven round inside the barrel at high speed. The next year, Wilkinson offered to make steam-engine cylinders, using the same machine, for Watt, who had just set up a business making steam engines in partnership with Matthew Boulton (1728–1809). Wilkinson's machine was just as successful in making steam-engine cylinders as it had been with cannon barrels. Wilkinson cylinders were used in the hundreds of Boulton and Watt steam engines which provided the power in the new factories that sprang up at the start of the Industrial Revolution.

ENERGY ON TAP

Once steam engines were available, manufacturers were quick to explore ways of using their tremendous and continuous power, a source of energy that had never been known before.

Henry Maudslay (1771–1831), another Englishman, invented an accurate screw-cutting lathe. In the past, large screws had been forged and then filed by hand to make the thread, while small screws were cut entirely by hand. This was slow and highly skilled work, and as a result screws were expensive. Maudslay's lathe meant that screws could be cut easily and accurately, with threads of standard sizes.

Maudslay's factory in London produced many other machine tools, but probably his most important other invention was the 'micrometer' for measuring machine parts with precision. This made use of the ability of his lathe to produce regular and accurate screw threads. The basis of the micrometer was a long screw with 20 threads to each centimetre, and pointers which could be moved by a thumbscrew up and down

The new mechanical lathe worked in much the same way as the pole lathe of the past, but was easier to control and more accurate.

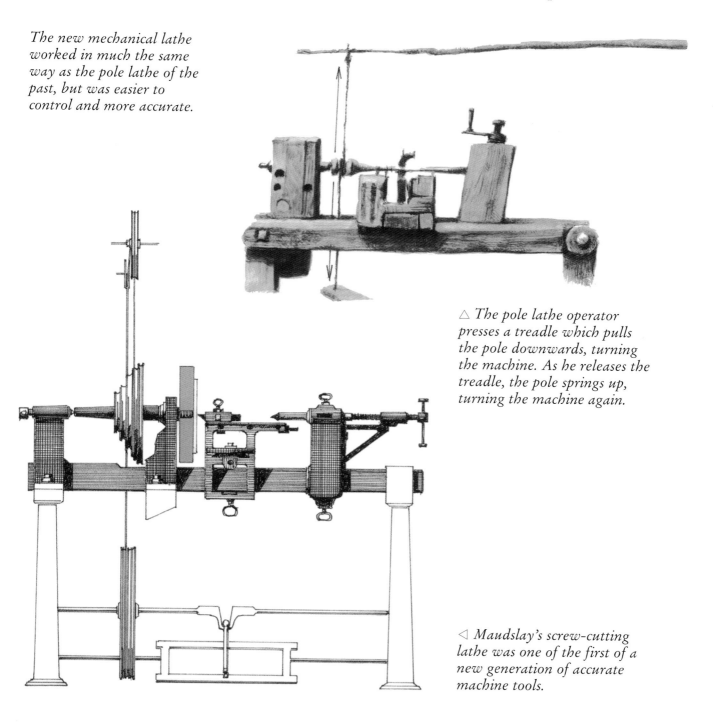

△ *The pole lathe operator presses a treadle which pulls the pole downwards, turning the machine. As he releases the treadle, the pole springs up, turning the machine again.*

◁ *Maudslay's screw-cutting lathe was one of the first of a new generation of accurate machine tools.*

the threads. Using this device, engineers could achieve a degree of accuracy unknown before.

STEAM PRESSURE

Scottish inventor, James Nasmyth (1808–90) invented the steam hammer in 1839, in which a weight was raised by steam pressure and then dropped on the piece of iron to be forged. The hammer was designed to forge a shaft for a new ship. The ship designer changed his plans, and the shaft was not needed, so this first Nasmyth hammer was never built. The drawings were seen and copied by a French iron founder, who built it at his works at Le Creuzot. Nasmyth went on to develop an even better steam hammer, which used steam to control the fall of the weight as well as to raise it.

The controls of the downward fall were so delicate that the hammer could be brought down on an egg so gently that the egg was cracked, but not broken. This trick was often performed to entertain and impress visitors.

The nineteenth century saw a flood of new machine tools for mechanizing a wide range of tasks. Rolling mills were designed for producing sheet metal. Punching machines and presses were built for such work as making coins and

medals. Other machines bent and formed metal into shapes. James Nasmyth invented machines for planing and cutting slots in metal. Mechanical saws and grinders, gear-cutters, wheel-cutters and many others added to the list of machine tools that produced work with a speed and accuracy never seen before.

THE WORLD'S WORKSHOP

Sparked off by the steam engine, the Industrial Revolution first took hold in Britain, and for years many of the major steps forward were made by British engineers and inventors. Britain became known as 'the workshop of the world', and talented engineers from other countries were attracted by the opportunities for progress.

One such man was Marc Isambard Brunel (1769–1849), a Frenchman who started a new career in England at the age of 30. He worked with Henry Maudslay on the development of machine tools that were used in naval dockyards and later became a pioneer in underwater tunnelling.

Brunel's son, Isambard Kingdom (1806–59), was one of the great railway-builders. French, Belgian and German manufacturers were keen to adopt British methods and machines; so much so, that, for a time, the British government banned the export of machinery to Europe to protect manufacturers at home.

Britain's leadership of the industrialized world was not to last. First the USA and later Germany began to catch up in the branches of industry where Britain had excelled. Both countries were also quicker to explore

◁ Nasmyth's steam hammer could be so accurately controlled that it could crack an egg without breaking it.

OUT OF WORK

The development of machine tools was good news for manufacturers, who could make their products in larger numbers, and for consumers, who could buy such things as clocks, furniture, cutlery and gardening tools more cheaply. It was not such good news for the skilled craft workers who had previously made these things by hand.

Many such people, in trades like spinning, weaving, metal grinding and cabinet-making, were thrown out of work by steam-driven spinning machines, looms and lathes. Their skills were not needed any more, and the only work they could find was as machine-minders in the factories, at lower rates of pay. One of the by-products of the Industrial Revolution was to make industrial workers less satisfied with their jobs and more resentful of the people who employed them.

the possibilities of two new sources of power which were eventually to take over from steam: electricity and the internal combustion engine.

American inventors such as Thomas Alva Edison (1847–1931) and Germans such as Ernst Werner von Siemens (1816–1892) were the leaders of the electrical revolution.

The internal combustion engine was the product of German engineers Gottlieb Daimler (1834–1900) and Karl Benz (1844–1929), with Rudolf Diesel (1853–1913) contributing the engine that still carries his name. These inventors of the machines of the modern age depended on the quest for quality and accuracy in machine tools by the engineers who preceded them.

NATURAL POWER

Blowing wind and flowing water are sources of energy that need no fuel and will never be used up. When people learned to tap this natural energy, they could begin to work more efficiently than ever before.

For thousands of years, people had only the power of their own muscles to help them with physical work such as carrying water, ploughing and building. As the first civilizations developed around farming communities and the first cities were built, there was an urgent need for human labour. Many early civilizations met this need by setting up systems of slavery.

One major goal of early wars was to bring back slaves from the conquered territories. Slave labour was responsible for the great building projects in ancient Egypt, Greece and Rome.

STEP BY STEP

Some machines were devised to make the best use of human effort. One of these was the treadmill, an open wheel fitted with steps and connected at the centre to a shaft. As slaves walked continuously inside the wheel, the shaft rotated and

△ *For thousands of years the only sources of power were the strength of a man or an animal.*

▷ *Slaves were valuable in the ancient world, because they were an important source of power.*

THE NORIA

The 'noria' was one of the earliest types of water wheel, which was probably used in the lands around the Mediterranean before the Roman Empire began to expand. The noria was a device for raising water from a river so that it could be channelled along ditches to irrigate the fields.

It was an undershot water wheel with paddles to catch the flow of water and jars fitted round the circumference. As the wheel turned anticlockwise in the flow of water, the jars were filled.

At the top of the cycle, the jars were emptied into the drainage channel.

could be used to drive machinery such as millstones and lifting devices.

Ox power was also available, but its use was limited to simple tasks such as pulling ploughs and operating water pumps. People had not yet started to use horses, so for most work people had to rely on themselves or their slaves.

There was a breakthrough during the first century BC, when water was used for the first time as a source of energy for grinding corn. The first water wheels had scoops or blades fitted to the end of a

vertical shaft. The top of the shaft passed through the centre of the lower of a pair of millstones and was attached to the upper stone. The blades at the other end were turned as river water flowed past them. Each complete turn of the shaft produced one complete turn of the upper millstone. This simple form of water-mill was first described by Greek writers, and is often called the Greek mill.

THE ROMAN WAY

The Greek mill worked, but it was not very efficient. It depended on a regular flow of water, so that any seasonal variation caused problems. Fortunately, improvements were on the way. The Romans had become experts in the use of water. They revolutionized the design of water mills by turning the wheel on its side and connecting it to the millstones using gears. In this way, the stones could be made to turn up to five times for each turn of the water wheel. The Roman design, with blades set across the wheel, made the maximum use of flowing water.

The Roman water wheel was 'undershot', which means that the water flowed beneath the blades. Undershot wheels had the disadvantage that if the river level dropped, the wheel turned slowly, or not at all. Later, people realized that if the water actually fell as it passed through the wheel, the power would be increased. The result was the 'breast' wheel, in which the water met the blades or buckets halfway down. The 'overshot' wheel, where the water flowed in at the top of the wheel, was a still later development. By this time, people had discovered how to provide a more regular supply of water by building a dam upstream and channelling the water to the wheel along a ditch or pipe.

It was only in the later days of their

empire that the Romans built water mills in large numbers, but some of these were very elaborate arrangements. At Barbegal, near Arles in France, they built a series of 16 wheels, each of which drove two pairs of millstones, making use, in turn, of the same flow of water. This mill could produce 28 tonnes of flour a day, enough to feed 80,000 people. The local population needed only a fraction of this, and the rest was probably sent away to feed the Roman army.

WATER FOR EVERYTHING

By the Middle Ages, water mills were being widely used in Europe, not only for grinding corn but also for powering saws, pounding rags to make paper, driving hammers for metal-working, hoisting stone and coal from quarries and mines, tanning leather and treating cloth.

Ownership of a corn mill was a profitable business. A landowner with a suitable river would build a water mill that farmers could use to grind their corn.

The fee they paid was usually a proportion of the flour produced, so that the owner had flour to sell without the trouble and expense of growing the corn himself. Monasteries were often the owners of large estates and they also went into the milling business.

There was a huge growth of water-mills in the late Middle Ages. In the Aube district of France, there were only

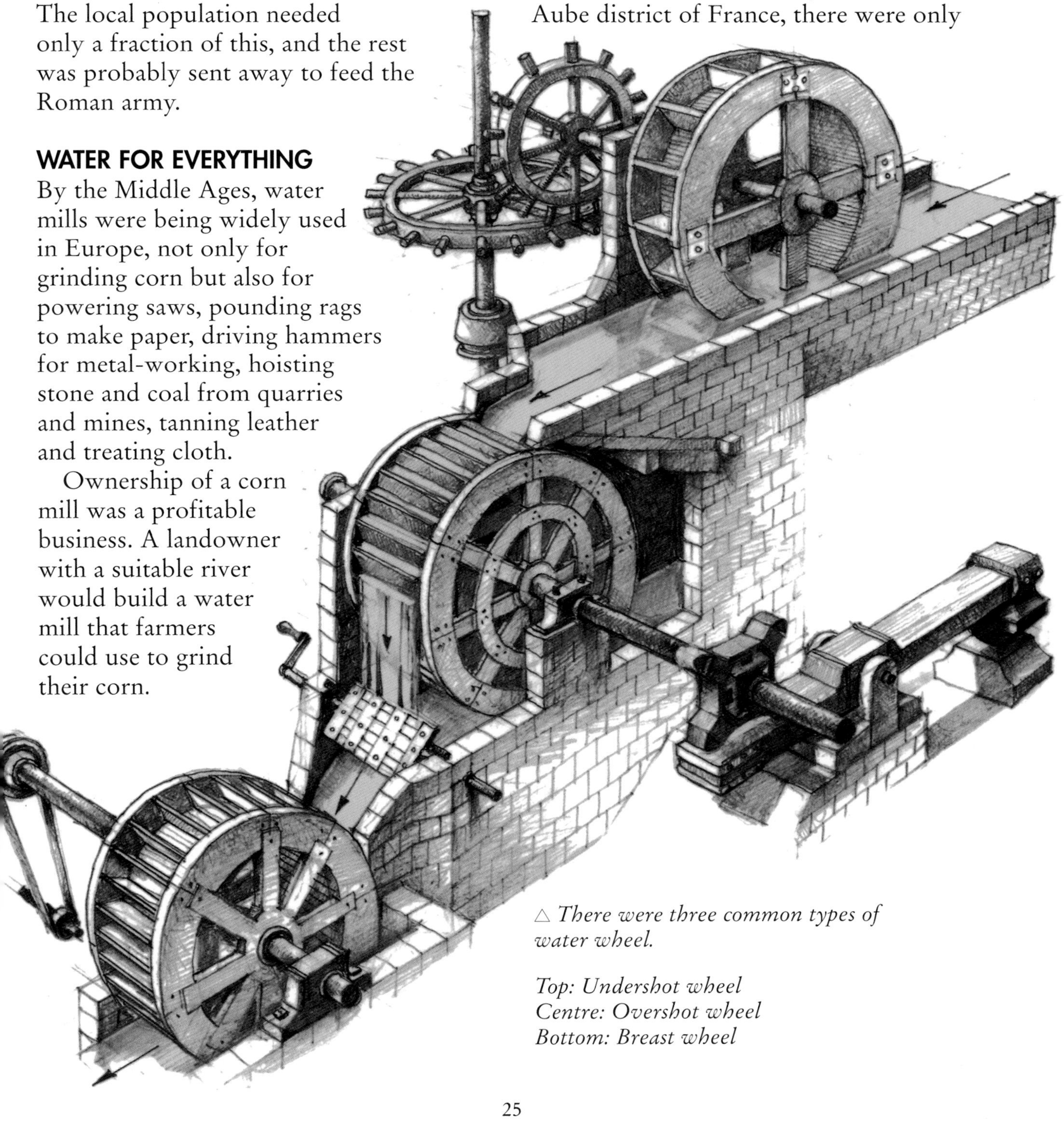

△ There were three common types of water wheel.

Top: Undershot wheel
Centre: Overshot wheel
Bottom: Breast wheel

NATURAL POWER

14 mills in the eleventh century. Less than two centuries later, there were 200. For communities fortunate enough to have been built on a fast-flowing river, water mills were the key to prosperity and growth. For example, by the sixteenth century, the Italian city of Bologna which lies at the foot of the Apennine Mountains had mills for grinding corn, metal-working, spinning, sawing, sharpening and polishing.

CATCHING THE WIND

Across the plains of Europe and central Asia and in the Middle East, fast-flowing rivers are far and few between. These were areas where the windmill became a popular source of natural power.

It was not until about AD 1100 that windmills were first built in Europe, but they had been used much earlier in China, Afghanistan and the Middle East.

▷ *Animals, the wind and water were sources of power that dominated the landscape for thousands of years.*

▽ *Gearing was needed to turn the motion of the water wheel from vertical into horizontal.*

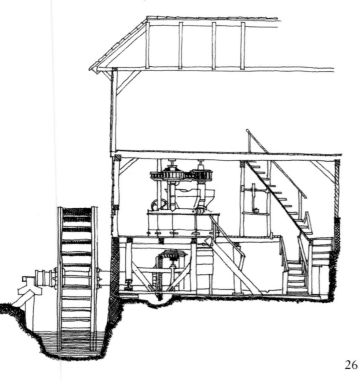

NATURAL POWER

The fact that the sails of early windmills often copied the local pattern of ship's sails, triangular in the Mediterranean and rectangular in China, suggests that the idea of using wind power on land may have come from its use at sea. In the first windmills, the sails travelled around in a horizontal path to drive a vertical shaft. An early example of this type of mill can still be seen at Seistan in Afghanistan, and similar designs are still in use in remote parts of the Middle East today. The Chinese, who use their windmills for irrigation, built the frames of bamboo so that they could be moved from place to place wherever irrigation was needed.

A traditional windmill from the Middle East.

WINDMILLS IN EUROPE

The idea of using wind power may have travelled from China or central Asia with traders returning from the Far East, or possibly through Russia and Scandinavia. However, it seems more likely that windmills in the West developed independently, as their design was, from the start, quite different from those in the East. The European windmill had a horizontal shaft driven by sails which moved in a vertical path. This first type of windmill was called a 'post mill'. The whole structure, built of wood, could be turned by human or animal power so that the sails faced into the wind.

The spread of windmills throughout Europe took place very quickly. Windmills could be built almost anywhere, although open hilltop sites were best. Building them required no great skill. Every community could have its own mill, and did not have to wait to have its corn ground at a water mill which might be miles away. Soon after the start of the twelfth century, there were hundreds and then thousands of windmills at work all over Europe.

The windmill was an invention that would last. For about 700 years, most people in Europe ate bread made from flour that had been ground by the wind. Going back 100 years, few pictures of a rural landscape in Europe did not include at least one windmill. Until about 60 years ago, there were many windmills in Europe still grinding corn. Even today, there are still a few at work, although they are now usually tourist attractions.

THE MOVING CAP

Improvements in the design of the windmill were introduced as time went on, though some communities continued to build the simple post mill. For most millers, however, the effort of constantly pushing the post mill into the wind was too much like hard work. The 'tower mill' or 'cap mill' made life easier.

The tower mill had a more substantial main structure which could be made of brick or stone. This contained the millstones and heavy machinery. The sails were attached to a wooden cap which was lighter and so easier to move into the wind. The effect of this was to raise the sails higher from the ground, catching

THE FAN MILL

The settlement of the great prairies of North America, Argentina and Australia in the nineteenth century led to the revival of the windmill in a new form. The 'fan mill', invented in the USA in 1850, was designed to pump water for use in isolated homesteads and cattle stations far from a piped water supply. The mill shown on the left was made by Australian settlers using the resources they found around them. Compare it to the strong stone European tower mill shown right.

The fan mill was light, cheaply produced, easy to transport and needed little maintenance. It was designed so that the blades could be adjusted, like a fan, to suit different strengths of wind. Millions of mills were produced in the USA and exported all over the world. By 1930, over six million were in use in the USA alone. Many are still at work around the world.

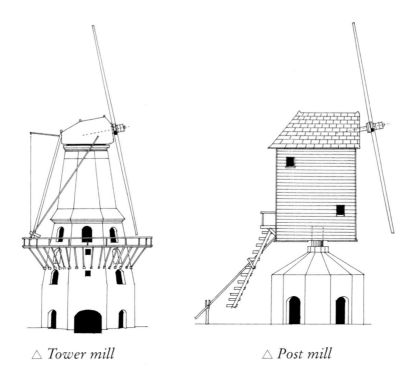

△ Tower mill   △ Post mill

in Britain and other countries.

The Dutch were also the first to use the wind to power sawmills, and the ease with which sawn timber could be produced resulted in the typical Dutch style of building in wood. The windmill had become the basic machine for many processes, from grinding exotic spices for the tables of the rich to grinding chalk to make whitewash for the walls of cottages. Even after the invention of the steam engine, it was hard to beat the economy and simplicity of wind power for these processes.

the wind better and also allowing other buildings such as store rooms and the miller's house to be built alongside. If the sails went out of control in high winds, as they often did, only the cap and not the whole mill would be damaged.

An important improvement was introduced in England in 1745 when a 'fantail' was added to a windmill. This was a smaller sail fitted opposite the main sails. The fantail caught the wind and automatically turned the main sails to face in the right direction. In countries like Britain, where the wind can change direction several times in the course of a day, this was a great help to the miller.

PUMPING AND SAWING

As with the water mill, it was soon found that windmills could perform a wide range of tasks. In the fifteenth century, the Dutch began to use windmills to pump water away from low-lying land. Later, they used them to reclaim new land from the sea, a method that was copied

THE RETURN OF THE WINDMILL

In many parts of the world, wind and water are still the most easily available sources of energy. Electricity has been generated from the flow of water through turbines in hydroelectric dams for almost 100 years, but until recently the possibility of using wind power was ignored. Wind generators, modern versions of the windmill, designed to generate electricity from rotating blades, have been brought into use and are supplying energy to national supply systems as well as isolated communities. It may be that we will once again come to value the source of energy that performed so many tasks for hundreds of years.

▷ *Today, natural power is becoming a valuable resource as people realize the polluting dangers of fossil fuels. Wind, water and solar power have all been developed to produce electricity.*

ELECTRIC POWER

For thousands of years, people wondered about the mysterious lightning they saw in the sky. Their questions revealed the existence of an energy source which is now available at the turn of a switch.

Electricity is part of the natural world. The first people only knew it in the form of lightning, a terrifying force that could destroy trees and buildings. The ancient Greeks noticed that rubbing amber, the fossilized gum from trees, made it attract light objects such as feathers or pieces of straw by a force we now know as 'static electricity'.

For centuries, both lightning and static electricity remained mysteries. No one suspected that they were examples of a form of energy that could be harnessed and used. In describing the effects of rubbing amber, the Greek scientist Thales of Miletus (624–565 BC) used the Greek word for amber, 'elektron'. The mysterious force now had a name.

THE ELECTRICITY-MAKERS

After about 1600, the study of science began to develop in Europe, and many scientists experimented with electricity. It was found that a machine in which a

△ *Benjamin Franklin, the great American scientist, proved that lightning is a form of electricity by flying a kite in a thunderstorm.*

THE LIGHTNING CONDUCTOR

A flash of lightning can contain over a million volts of electrical energy producing temperatures as high as 30,000 degrees Celsius. This enormous energy is seeking the most direct way to the ground. When it does so, it can do great damage to trees and buildings and cause fires.

The lightning conductor, invented by Benjamin Franklin, is based on the simple idea of providing lightning with a direct route to the ground. The conductor is a copper rod fixed to the highest point of a building. A strong cable leads down from the rod and is buried deep in the ground. If lightning strikes, it hits the highest point on the building, the conductor. The energy travels down the cable to the ground harmlessly, while the building is unaffected.

piece of cloth rubbed continuously against a glass plate could produce a flow or 'current' of electricity. Pieter van Musschenbroek (1692–1761), the professor of physics at Leyden University in the Netherlands, discovered, in 1746, that an electric current produced in this way could be stored for a short time in a jar of water and that the spark from it could give an electric shock. His device became known as the Leyden jar.

The next important piece of understanding about electricity came from the United States. Benjamin Franklin (1706–90) was an American statesman who had many other interests, one of which was science. He was particularly fascinated by electricity. It was Franklin who first proved that lightning was a form of electricity.

During a thunderstorm in 1752, Benjamin Franklin carried out an

Hans Christian Oersted

ELECTRICAL UNITS

Hans Christian Oersted, Alessandro Volta, Michael Faraday and other pioneers of electricity are remembered in the names given to units and measurements of electricity. An oersted is a unit by which magnetic force is measured. The strength of an electric current is measured in volts. Electromagnetic units are measured in farads, named after Michael Faraday.

Other scientists whose names are remembered in electrical terms include George Simon Ohm (1789–1854), whose name is given to the unit of electrical resistance, and André Marie Ampère. One ampere, or amp, is the amount of current that one volt can send through a resistance of one ohm.

Strangely enough, the electrical term which is used most often takes the name of James Watt, the steam engine pioneer who died in 1819 just before the age of electricity began. The watt is the unit that measures the rate at which electricity is generated or used.

experiment. He flew a kite into the storm clouds, with a key tied to the end of the string. Lightning hit the kite, and a current of static electricity flowed down the string into the key, and from the key to the ground, causing a series of sparks. Franklin then connected the kite to a Leyden jar, and found that the water in the jar became electrically charged.

Franklin also worked out that there were negative and positive electrical charges, which caused sparks when they were brought together.

Another university professor who became interested in electricity was an Italian, Alessandro Volta (1745–1827). Working at the University of Pavia in northern Italy, he invented a number of devices for storing electricity. One was the 'electrophorus', which produced a charge of electricity in a metal plate held above a charged piece of ebonite, a hard substance made from rubber.

THE BATTERY

Volta's next step was to produce the 'Voltaic pile', the first chemical battery for storing electricity. It consisted of a number of copper and zinc discs separated by paper soaked in acid. A later version had sheets of copper and zinc placed in an acid solution. The sheets were connected above the solution by wire, and a continuous electric current flowed along it.

Although the development of the convenient battery that we know today was many years ahead, Volta's experiments demonstrated the principle on which they work. As yet, however, no one had any idea of how electricity could be put to use.

▷ *Alessandro Volta experimenting with the Voltaic pile.*

◁ *Michael Faraday holds up a magnet with wire coiled around it. The electrical current generated in the wire was the first electrical motor. On the table are two early generators.*

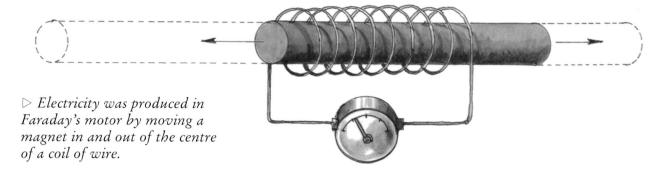

▷ *Electricity was produced in Faraday's motor by moving a magnet in and out of the centre of a coil of wire.*

MAKING ELECTRICITY WORK

Explanations of electricity were slowly being gathered together. Another contributor to this understanding was a Danish scientist, Hans Christian Oersted (1777–1851). In 1820, he discovered the link between electricity and magnetism. He found that when a compass was placed near a wire carrying an electric current, the compass needle moved. This was a very significant discovery. It showed that electrical energy could be converted into mechanical energy. Electricity could make things move.

A French physicist, André Marie Ampère (1775–1836), followed up Oersted's experiments and made a further discovery. The whole area around the current-carrying wire had a magnetic effect. Ampère called this the 'magnetic field'. At the time, this seemed like just another interesting fact about electricity. However, it was a discovery that led to the development of the electric motor.

The scientist who made the breakthrough was Englishman Michael Faraday (1791–1867). In 1821, he set up an experiment in which an electric current was passed between two beakers of mercury, each containing a bar magnet. When the current was flowing, one of the bar magnets began to rotate round the wire in its beaker. In the other beaker, the magnet was fixed, and the wire rotated round the magnet. When the current was switched off, the movement stopped.

Like all good scientists, Michael Faraday was forever asking questions. His 1821 experiment had used electricity to produce magnetism, which in turn produced movement. Could magnetism, he asked himself, produce electricity? In 1831, he found the answer.

THE FIRST ELECTRIC MOTOR

Faraday made a coil of wire around a magnet, and found that the magnet induced, or brought about, a current in the coil. Almost as soon as it was induced, the current stopped, but if the magnet was removed a current was induced again, this time in the opposite direction. So if the magnet was moved in and out of the coil, a continuous current, running first one way and then the other, was the result. This kind of electricity, called 'alternating current', is the kind that is supplied to our houses by power stations. Faraday had made the discovery that made electricity a useful source of power.

As often happens when people in different places are working along the same lines, an American scientist, Joseph Henry (1797–1878), had made the same discovery as Faraday at about the same time. It happened that Faraday was the first to publish details of his experiments, and, as a result, his name is better known.

INVENTORS TAKE A HAND

Scientists are usually interested in how and why things happen. They are less interested in turning what they have discovered to practical use. This was so with Faraday and Henry. For example, Henry suggested that his work could lead to the electric telegraph, but he did not follow this up himself. Similarly, Faraday did not go on to produce a dynamo or generator to make a continuous supply of electricity. What happened at this point was that various people, almost all of them outside universities, began to use the scientists' discoveries to invent the major electrical devices. In Belgium, Zenobe Theophile Gramme (1826–1901) made the first generator producing 'direct current'. In the USA, Samuel Morse (1791–1872) produced the first successful electric telegraph system. Working separately, Britain's Joseph Swan (1828–1914) and the USA's Thomas Alva Edison developed the electric light bulb.

The new electrical devices worked, and there was a demand for them, but who was going to supply the electricity? Should every home and factory, or every street, have its own

▷ *Edison's light bulb was lit by passing an electric current through a carbon filament within a vacuum.*

generator? Could electricity be supplied from some central point, in the same way as water was piped from the waterworks to every building in the district?

The idea of supplying electricity to a district from a power station seems obvious to us, but in the 1880s it was not as straightforward as it seems today. One problem was the expense of laying miles of copper cable to carry the supply. Another was that most towns and cities already had gas supplies piped beneath their streets which were used for lighting, heating and cooking in homes, and the gas companies did not welcome rivals for their business. Most challenging of all, there were technical problems, one of which was that a large amount of energy was lost as the electricity travelled along the cables.

MAKING CONNECTIONS

Thomas Edison was not only an inventor. He was also a businessman, keen to make money out of his inventions. Soon after he had produced his first successful electric light bulb in 1879, he began to plan a district power system. He designed his own cables and circuits, a new generator which was more efficient than previous models, and even a meter to record how much electricity consumers used.

The Edison Electric Light Company built a power station at Pearl Street, in New York's Manhattan district, and wired up offices and buildings within the area. At 3.00 pm on 4 September 1882, the electric power was switched on for the first time.

RIVAL SYSTEMS

Revolutionary and exciting though Edison's Pearl Street scheme was, more work was needed before electricity generation was efficient enough to supply a whole town or city. One question that had to be settled was whether direct current (DC) or alternating current (AC) should be used. Edison's was a direct current system. It transmitted a low voltage current which was particularly prone to the loss of energy.

Joseph Swan

Another American engineer, George Westinghouse (1846–1914) developed a rival AC system, based on the discovery that high voltage current lost far less energy in transmission. In the Westinghouse system, electricity was transmitted at a high voltage which was then reduced to a safer, lower voltage before it reached the consumer.

The key device in this system was the 'transformer', invented in 1885 by a New York engineer, William Stanley (1858–1916). This increased the voltage of electricity leaving the power station for transmission along the cables. A second transformer decreased the voltage to a safe level for use. The transformer, which works only with alternating current, consists of two coils of wire wound around an iron core. It enables the voltage of the current entering one of the coils to be increased or decreased according to the number of turns in each coil.

For some years, the Edison and Westinghouse systems were rivals. As more electrical devices were invented, including electric trains, which first appeared in Germany in 1879, it became clear that both AC and DC had their

▽ *Edison's 'invention factory' at his home at Menlo Park.*

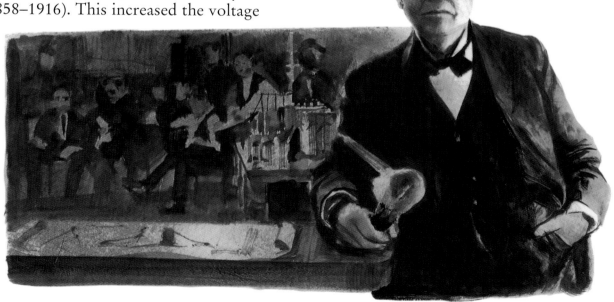

AC/DC
The difference between direct current and alternating current is easy to remember.

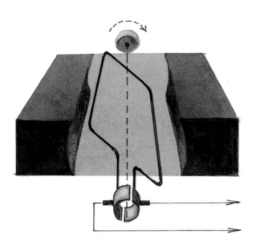

Direct current is the kind produced by a battery. The electricity flows in only one direction, along the positive wire and back through the negative.

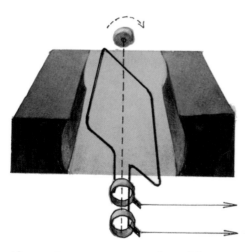

Alternating current, produced by a dynamo or generator, is the kind delivered by public electricity supply systems. The direction in which alternating current flows changes 120 times every second, 60 times in one direction and 60 times in the other.

particular uses. Edison lost interest in electricity and moved on to other inventions. Meanwhile, one of his chief engineers, Croatian-born Nicola Tesla (1856–1943), quarrelled with him and left to join Westinghouse. Tesla was an enthusiast for AC systems, and the partnership between him and Westinghouse shaped the future of the electricity supply industry.

In 1893, the Westinghouse company provided the electricity supply for the World's Fair in Chicago with a system that could supply both AC and DC, at different voltages for different purposes.

HYDROELECTRICITY
Two years later, there was another triumph for Westinghouse. In 1885, the world's first hydroelectric power station, generating electricity from the energy of falling water, had been opened in France, and other stations in Europe followed. George Westinghouse's plan was to harness the power of one of the world's most famous waterfalls, Niagara, on the border of the United States and Canada.

The scheme was a huge success. The Niagara Falls power station produced enough energy for local needs and supplied the industrial town of Buffalo, 32 kilometres away. Hydroelectricity had proved itself, and became a major source of energy in countries where heavy rainfall and mountainous terrain make it possible.

THE STEAM TURBINE
Elsewhere, electricity had to be made by raising steam to drive the generator. The first generators were heavy, noisy and vibrated so badly that the buildings housing them had to be very strong.

In 1884, a British engineer, Charles Parsons (1854–1931), demonstrated the

▽ *A hydroelectric power station harnesses the force of a flowing waterfall and turns it into electricity.*

lighter and more efficient steam turbine which was to become standard generating equipment. The steam turbine contains sets of thin blades mounted on a shaft. Steam is forced at high pressure through the blades, making the shaft rotate. The steam is raised in a boiler by burning coal, oil or gas, or by using nuclear fuel.

ELECTRICITY FOR EVERYONE

By 1900, everything was in place for the development of the electricity supply industry of today. William Stanley had gone on to work on systems for transmitting electricity over greater and greater distances. A German-born American, Charles Proteus Steinmetz (1865–1923), also contributed by working out how AC circuits work and by inventing a device which limited lightning damage to transmission lines. The erection of transmission lines across the country enabled electricity to be generated at power stations close to their source of fuel, which in turn cut the price of energy by greatly reducing fuel transport costs.

Every industrialized country now has its chain of power stations connected with consumers through a network of high voltage cables, bringing light and power even to remote communities.

NUCLEAR POWER

A scientific quest to find the smallest particle of matter led to the discovery of an energy source with the ability to supply a large part of the world's energy needs, or to destroy the world altogether.

Until less than 100 years ago, scientists believed that the atom was the smallest particle of matter and it was the basic building block from which everything was made. This idea was put forward about 400 BC in ancient Greece, and had remained unchallenged ever since.

In 1897, a British scientist, Joseph John Thompson (1856–1940), reported that in his experiments he had observed smaller units of matter that he called 'electrons'. This led to the realization that each atom was made up of a number of smaller, or 'subatomic' particles.

POSITIVE AND NEGATIVE

At that time two different types of particles were identified, 'protons' and 'electrons', but a third type, 'neutrons', was added later. Protons are particles carrying a positive electrical charge, and they are found in the 'nucleus' or core of the atom. Orbiting round the nucleus are negatively charged particles called

△ *Rutherford's apparatus for splitting nitrogen atoms.*

1896 Antoine Becquerel (1852–1908) discovers that uranium emits invisible radiation.

1900 Max Planck (1858–1947) develops the 'quantum theory', that energy exists in small, exact units.

1913 Neils Bohr (1885–1962) describes the atom as a nucleus with orbiting electrons.

1919 Ernest Rutherford deduces the presence of the atom's nucleus.

electrons. Neutrons, which carry no charge at all, were not identified until 1932 by James Chadwick (1891–1974), although Ernest Rutherford (1871–1937) had earlier said that they existed in the nucleus of the atom. These discoveries meant that, theoretically, the nucleus of an atom could be divided into two or more parts by a process called 'fission'.

This discovery completely overturned the physicists' view of the world they thought they understood, but another shock was yet to come. In 1906, the Swiss physicist Albert Einstein (1879– 1955) published his theory that energy and matter were different forms of the same thing, and that each could be converted to the other, and back again.

THE SECRET OF URANIUM-235
So far, this was all theory, but the possibilities that lay behind it were enormous. Just how enormous became clearer when a group of scientists began working with atoms of the element uranium. Uranium atoms occur in three different types or 'isotopes' with varying numbers of neutrons inside them.

In 1938, three physicists began experimenting in Berlin, Germany, with the isotope called uranium-235. They were a German, Otto Hahn (1879–1968), and two Austrians, Lise Meitner

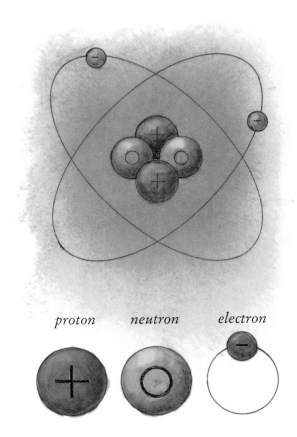

proton   neutron   electron

◁ *The structure of the atom.*

1932 James Chadwick discovers neutrons in the nuclei of atoms.

1939 Otto Hahn produces the first nuclear fission reaction.

1939 Lise Meitner produces energy from nuclear fission.

1942 Enrico Fermi creates the first nuclear reactor.

(1878–1968) and Otto Frisch (1904–79). They found that if an atom of uranium-235 is bombarded with neutrons it undergoes fission. It breaks down into two equal parts, with two or three neutrons left over. These neutrons act on other uranium atoms, causing them to break up. This effect is called a 'chain reaction' and releases a great deal of energy. A chain reaction in which all the nuclei in a piece of uranium explode in a split second results in a devastating explosion.

THE NUCLEAR BOMB
In 1939, World War II broke out and, immediately, both sides stepped up their research with the aim of being the first to produce a bomb which made use of the chain reaction caused

by splitting uranium-235 atoms.

In the USA, Leo Szilard (1898–1964) and Enrico Fermi (1901–54) managed to create a controlled, continuous source of nuclear energy, a 'nuclear reactor' in 1942. In August 1945, the world awoke to the significance of this work when American Air Force planes dropped nuclear bombs on Hiroshima and Nagasaki in Japan, so bringing World War II to an end.

When peace came, scientists turned their attention to the peaceful uses of nuclear energy. The first working nuclear power station was opened at Calder Hall in northern England in 1956. It used the heat produced by a nuclear reaction to create steam which

◁ *Nuclear fission*

44

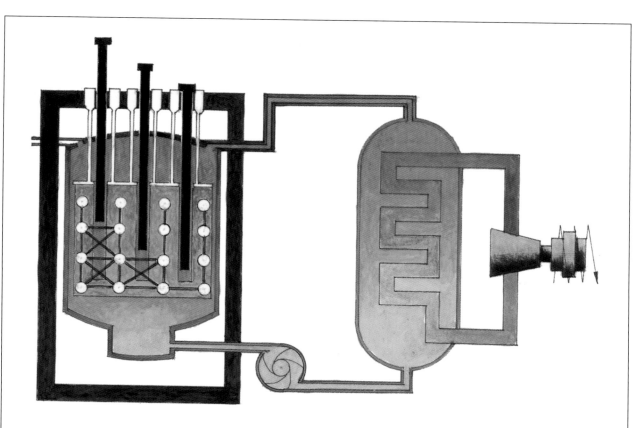

HOW A NUCLEAR REACTOR WORKS

There are several different types of nuclear reactor in use in power stations. The type in the diagram above is called a 'thermal reactor'. The reactor itself is a large concrete vessel into which rods of uranium are lowered from the top. Tremendous heat is generated when streams of neutrons strike the uranium and split its atoms. Hot gases are channelled to a boiler where they are used to create steam, which then drives a turbine. Meanwhile, the cool gas is returned to the reactor to be heated again. Control rods, which absorb the stream of neutrons and prevent it from reaching the uranium, are used to slow down the reaction or stop it altogether.

was then used to drive steam turbines to produce electricity.

THE PRICE OF POWER

By 1986, there were over 370 nuclear power stations in the world, with many more being built. However, in that year something happened which gave the world a dramatic warning of how easily nuclear power could lead to disaster.

One April night, engineers at the Chernobyl power station in the Ukraine ignored safety rules and allowed the station's nuclear reactor to heat up out of control. The reactor exploded, creating radioactive dust which was carried on the wind and affected human, animal and plant life across a wide area of north-western Europe.

Thousands of farm animals had to be destroyed, while, closer to Chernobyl, the number of people who will die young as a result of the radioactive fallout, may never be known. It was a grim reminder that, although nuclear reactors can provide the world with energy that it desperately needs, the price of this energy must be total safety.

FIND OUT SOME MORE

After you have read about the ideas and inventions in this book, you may want to find out some more information about them. There are lots of books devoted to specific topics, such as electricity or machines, so that you can discover more facts. All over Britain and Ireland, you can see historical sites and visit museums that contain historical artefacts that will tell you more about the subjects that interest you. The books, sites and museums listed below cover some of the most important topics in this book. They are just a start!

GENERAL INFORMATION
BOOKS

These books all present a large number of inventions of all different kinds:

Oxford Illustrated Encyclopedia of Invention and Technology edited by Sir Monty Finniston (Oxford University Press, 1992)

Usborne Illustrated Handbook of Invention and Discovery by Struan Reid (Usborne, 1986)

Invention by Lionel Bender (Dorling Kindersley, 1986)

The Way Things Work by David Macaulay (Dorling Kindersley, 1988)

Key Moments in Science and Technology by Keith Wicks (Hamlyn, 1999)

A History of Invention by Trevor I. Williams (Little Brown, 1999)

WEBSITE

For information on many different inventions, visit: http://inventors.about.com

MUSEUMS

Many large museums contain interesting artefacts related to people of the past, and some have collections that may be more specifically about some of the themes covered in this book.

To find out more about the museums in your area, ask in your local library or tourist information office, or look in the telephone directory.

A useful guide is *Museums & Galleries in Great Britain & Ireland* (British Leisure Publications, East Grinstead) which tells you about over 1,300 places to visit. For a good introduction to the subjects covered in this book, visit:

Science Museum, Exhibition Road, London SW7
www.sciencemuseum.org.uk

For displays and information about many of the earliest ideas and inventions, go to:

British Museum, Great Russell Street, London WC1
www.britishmuseum.co.uk

MACHINES
MUSEUMS

The science of levers, pulleys and other simple machines, plus demonstrations of their practical uses, is a subject covered by many museums all over the country. You could visit:

Eureka!, Discovery Road, Halifax, West Yorkshire
www.eureka.org.uk

Museum of the History of Science, Broad Street, Oxford
www.mhs.oxac.uk
A collection of early scientific and medical instruments.

NATURAL POWER
BOOKS

Windmills by Althea and Edward Parker (A & C Black, 1992)

SITES

Working water and windmills can be seen all over the country. There is an outstanding watermill at **Quarry Bank Mill**, Styal, Wilmslow, Cheshire (www.quarrybankmill.org.uk). One of the best mills is **Bourn Mill**, Cambridgeshire (www.cpswandlebury.demon.co.uk). For a local mill or watermill, ask in your tourist information office or library. You could also visit:

Centre for Alternative Technology, near Machynlleth, Powys, Wales
www.cat.org.uk
Fascinating displays of solar, water and wind power all put to practical use.

Museum of Waterpower, Finch Foundry, Sticklepath, near Okehampton, Devon

POWER
MUSEUMS

Science Museum, London (address above)

Michael Faraday's Laboratory, The Royal Institution, 21 Albemarle St, London W1
www.rigb.org

Kelham Island Industrial Museum, Alma Street, Sheffield S3, South Yorks
www.simt.co.uk/kel1
This museum includes the world's largest working steam engine.

SITES

Power stations around the country usually have open days when you can visit. To find out about them, ask in your local tourist information office.

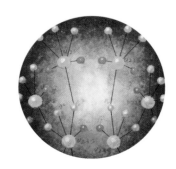

INDEX

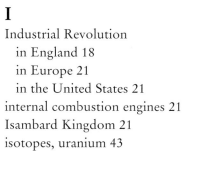
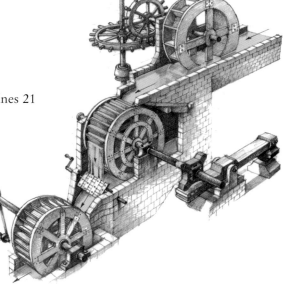

INDEX